Stupid Graphic Designer Jokes

Stupid Graphic Designer Jokes

R.K. REID

Copyright © 2025 R.K. Reid
All rights reserved.

ISBN: 9798262013401

Disclaimer

This is a humor and parody book meant for entertainment only.

The author and publisher take no responsibility for hurt feelings, bruised egos, or sudden awareness of questionable career choices.

Graphic Designers:
We joke because we care…

Dedication

To my beloved and ever-entertaining furry friends, Mr. Chai and Maile, this book is dedicated to you both.

Your playful antics and unwavering support have inspired this collection of silly one-liner jokes.

Your mischievous charms & naughty antics will always be remembered.

I always love you guys!

A Message for You

To: _____

From: _____

Date: _____

A note from your gift giver:

_____

_____

_____

_____

_____

May this book bring you lots of laughs and brighten your day!

What on Earth should I scribble down on this page?

This book template seems to have run out of creative juice.

Perhaps I can seize this opportunity to shamelessly promote my website.

Hey there! Take a gander at my marvelous online realm:

www.stupidjokebooks.com

Prepare yourself for an extraordinary experience with my breathtaking selection of "Stupid" joke books.

Caution: Excessive laughter and inevitable disappointment await!

Contents

Jokes	5
More Jokes	10
More Jokes	17
More Jokes	33
More Jokes	37
More Jokes	45
More Jokes	51
More Jokes	63
More Jokes	77
More Jokes	113

(Jokes On You!)

(There Are No Page Numbers!)

"Graphic designers don't argue — they just passive-aggressively change the font."

Why do graphic designers always look happy when clients approve the first draft?

Because they know the client will ask for 47 revisions tomorrow.

Fun Fact: Studies show that 89.3% of graphic designers develop permanent smile lines from fake enthusiasm during client presentations.

What do graphic designers and octopi have in common?

They both need eight arms to handle all the projects clients dump on them.

Fun Fact: Marine biologists report that octopi have better time management skills than most freelance designers.

How can you tell a graphic designer is having a breakdown?

Their coffee mug says "World's Okayest Designer" instead of "Creative Genius."

Fun Fact: Coffee scientists classify graphic designers as the only species that can photosynthesize pure caffeine.

What's the difference between a smartphone and a graphic designer?

The smartphone actually responds when you try to update it.

Fun Fact: Tech support reports that smartphones crash less frequently than designers' Adobe Creative Suite.

Why don't bears make good graphic designers?

They can't handle the hibernation period between project brief and final payment.

Fun Fact: Zoologists use graphic designers to test bear patience levels during winter research.

What's more reliable than a pizza delivery estimate?

A graphic designer's project timeline - both are complete fiction.

Fun Fact: Pizza delivery drivers report better accuracy rates than designers estimating revision counts.

How is a graphic designer's creativity like their phone battery?

Both die right when you need them most for an important presentation.

Fun Fact: Energy researchers found that designer creativity drains faster than any known battery technology.

What's the only crown a graphic designer will ever wear?

The one made of crumpled rejection letters and unpaid invoices.

Fun Fact: Royal historians confirm that actual crowns require less maintenance than designer egos.

Why do graphic designers hoard toilet paper like it's gold?

Because they're used to clients treating their work the same way.

Fun Fact: Economists report that toilet paper has maintained more stable value than designer hourly rates.

Why do aliens never abduct graphic designers?

Even extraterrestrials can't figure out what they actually do for work.

Fun Fact: NASA uses graphic designers to confuse potential alien visitors and protect Earth's location.

What's the most useless tool in a graphic designer's arsenal?

Their calculator - they never charge enough anyway.

Fun Fact: Mathematics professors study graphic designers to understand how humans can survive without basic arithmetic.

What killed the dinosaurs before the meteor?

They tried to explain vector graphics to a T-Rex client.

Fun Fact: Paleontologists believe dinosaurs went extinct because they couldn't adapt to revision requests.

When do graphic designers break out the wine glasses?

When the client finally pays... or when they give up and become alcoholics.

Fun Fact: Sommeliers report that graphic designers have the most sophisticated taste in cheap wine.

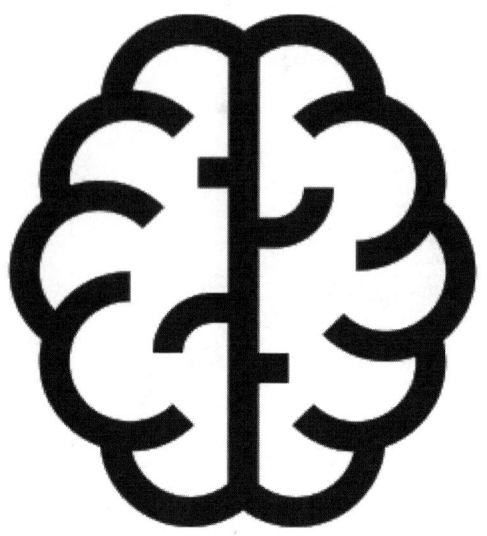

What's smaller than a graphic designer's brain after 10 revisions?

Their remaining will to live and their bank account balance.

Fun Fact: Neuroscientists use graphic designers to study how creativity gradually deteriorates under pressure.

Why are graphic designers terrible at soccer?

They spend too much time perfecting the logo and forget to play the game.

Fun Fact: FIFA banned graphic designers from designing balls because they kept adding drop shadows.

What's more mythical than a unicorn?

A graphic designer who gets paid on time without doing revisions.

Fun Fact: Fantasy authors study graphic designers to create believable impossible creatures.

Why did NASA hire graphic designers for the space program?

They're the only humans who can make something take forever to launch.

Fun Fact: Aerospace engineers report that rocket launches are faster than designer project deliveries.

What does a graphic designer see in the mirror?

Someone who definitely should have gone to business school instead.

Fun Fact: Psychologists use mirrors to help graphic designers practice saying "no" to unreasonable requests.

How hot does a graphic designer's temper get?

About as hot as their laptop running Adobe Creative Suite.

Fun Fact: Meteorologists use graphic designers' stress levels to predict weather patterns.

What's the difference between a hamburger and a graphic design project?

The hamburger actually gets finished and consumed within a reasonable timeframe.

Fun Fact: Fast food chains hire graphic designers to make wait times feel shorter by comparison.

Why do graphic designers make great ghosts?

They're already experts at haunting clients who don't pay invoices.

Fun Fact: Paranormal investigators report that graphic designers make the most persistent spirits.

What's the most expensive piece of paper a graphic designer owns?

Their art school diploma that qualified them for minimum wage freelancing.

Fun Fact: Universities use graphic design programs to test how much debt students can accumulate.

Why are graphic designers like broken bicycles?

They look functional but can't handle any real workload.

Fun Fact: Bicycle mechanics report better job satisfaction rates than graphic designers.

What magical power do all graphic designers wish they had?

The ability to make clients understand why Comic Sans is not appropriate.

Fun Fact: Magicians study graphic designers to learn advanced disappearing acts with deadlines.

When do graphic designers cry tears of joy?

When they realize their student loan payments are finally larger than their rent.

Fun Fact: Emotional researchers use graphic designers to study the full spectrum of human despair.

Why are graphic designers like avocados?

They're trendy, overpriced, and go bad right when you need them most.

Fun Fact: Nutritionists report that avocados have more stable shelf life than designer motivation.

What's a graphic designer's worst nightmare?

A client with 20/20 vision who actually notices their mistakes.

Fun Fact: Optometrists recommend graphic designers to patients who need practice ignoring obvious problems.

How many graphic designers does it take to change a light bulb?

Twelve - one to change it and eleven to argue about the font on the packaging.

Fun Fact: Electrical engineers study graphic designers to understand how humans function without bright ideas.

What's the difference between a monkey and a junior graphic designer?

The monkey eventually stops flinging things when it doesn't get bananas.

Fun Fact: Primatologists use graphic designers to demonstrate evolutionary regression in action.

Why don't graphic designers rob banks?

They'd spend six months perfecting the heist logo and miss the actual crime.

Fun Fact: Bank security systems are designed by graphic designers because they're guaranteed to be unnecessarily complex.

What trophy do graphic designers win most often?

"Most Creative Excuse for Missing a Deadline" three years running.

Fun Fact: Awards committees created separate categories for graphic designers because they dominated the procrastination prizes.

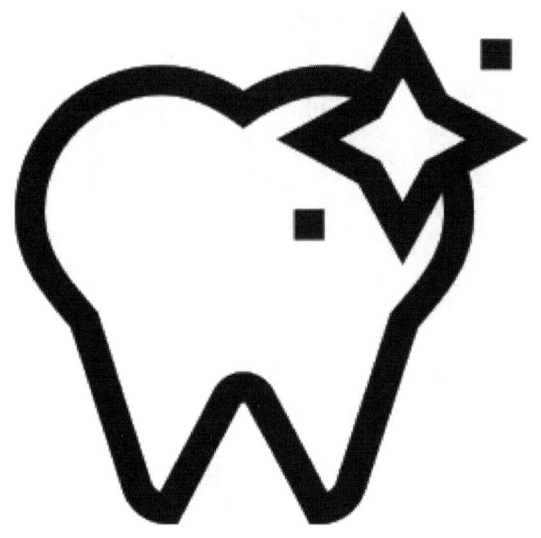

Why are graphic designers like wisdom teeth?

Painful to deal with, expensive to remove, and you question why they exist.

Fun Fact: Dentists recommend graphic designers to patients who need practice enduring prolonged suffering.

How is graphic design like swimming?

You can drown in both, and lifeguards won't save you from either.

Fun Fact: Olympic swimmers report better stroke consistency than graphic designers maintain style guides.

What's a graphic designer's favorite target practice?

Missing every single client deadline while somehow hitting their caffeine goals.

Fun Fact: Archery instructors use graphic designers to demonstrate how to consistently miss the point.

Why can't graphic designers afford houses?

They keep spending their down payments on the latest Adobe subscription updates.

Fun Fact: Real estate agents use graphic designers as examples of why renting is sometimes permanent.

What time is it when a graphic designer says they'll be done "soon"?

Time to find a new designer because "soon" means next calendar year.

Fun Fact: Clockmakers study graphic designers to understand how time can theoretically move backwards.

Why are dogs better employees than graphic designers?

Dogs actually come when called and don't charge by the hour.

Fun Fact: Veterinarians report that dogs show more loyalty than designers show to brand guidelines.

How is a graphic designer's work ethic like a broken car?

Lots of noise about starting up, but it never actually goes anywhere.

Fun Fact: Automotive engineers use graphic designers to test customer patience with unreliable products.

Why don't graphic designers make good birthday cakes?

They'd charge extra for each candle and redesign the frosting seventeen times.

Fun Fact: Bakers report that birthday cakes have better deadline management than graphic design projects.

What's the leading cause of graphic designer hospital visits?

Repetitive stress injury from constantly pressing Ctrl+Z on their life choices.

Fun Fact: Emergency rooms stock extra tissues specifically for graphic designers having creative breakdowns.

What's a graphic designer's relationship with money?

Like a bad Tinder date - brief contact, high expectations, inevitable disappointment.

Fun Fact: Financial advisors use graphic designers as examples of how not to manage money.

Why do graphic designers work best at night?

Because that's when normal people can't see their questionable design choices.

Fun Fact: Astronomers report that the moon has more consistent phases than graphic designer sleep schedules.

What melts faster than ice cream in summer?

A graphic designer's confidence during a client presentation.

Fun Fact: Dairy scientists use graphic designers to study rapid deterioration under pressure.

Why don't graphic designers use wrenches?

They prefer to screw things up digitally rather than mechanically.

Fun Fact: Mechanics report that wrenches are more reliable tools than graphic designers are reliable contractors.

What's the difference between a microphone and a graphic designer?

The microphone only amplifies sound, not excuses.

Fun Fact: Audio engineers prefer working with feedback over working with graphic designer feedback.

Why are graphic designers always running?

Usually away from deadlines, toward coffee shops, or from angry clients.

Fun Fact: Marathon trainers use graphic designers to demonstrate improper running form and poor endurance.

What's the most productive tool in a designer's studio?

The trash can - it's where their best ideas go after client feedback.

Fun Fact: Waste management companies report that graphic designers generate 73% more crumpled paper than other professions.

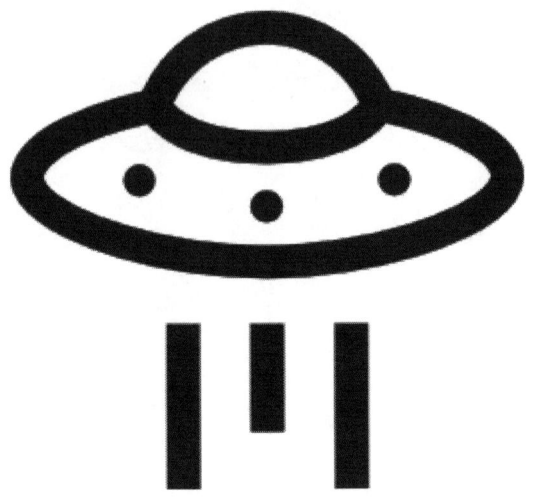

Why do UFOs never hire graphic designers?

Even aliens know better than to trust someone who thinks lens flares solve everything.

Fun Fact: Extraterrestrial research shows that alien civilizations collapsed after hiring their first graphic designers.

How is making a sandwich like working with a graphic designer?

You order turkey, get mystery meat, and pay premium prices for basic ingredients.

Fun Fact: Sandwich artists report better customer satisfaction ratings than graphic designers.

What's inside every graphic designer's briefcase?

Unpaid invoices, broken dreams, and a backup application to art school.

Fun Fact: Business professionals use graphic designers as examples of how not to present yourself professionally.

Why do graphic designers still own pencils?

To stab themselves when clients suggest "making the logo bigger."

Fun Fact: Pencil manufacturers report that graphic designers purchase more erasers than actual graphite.

When does a graphic designer's phone show full battery?

Never - just like their bank account and their patience with clients.

Fun Fact: Battery manufacturers study graphic designers to develop technology that drains faster than professional motivation.

What do graphic designers pray for most?

Clients who understand the difference between "creative input" and "total redesign."

Fun Fact: Religious leaders report that graphic designers have the most specific prayer requests in recorded history.

Why are graphic designers like theater masks?

They're always performing emotions they don't actually feel for their audience.

Fun Fact: Drama teachers use graphic designers to demonstrate method acting in real-world applications.

What's the only thing a graphic designer can fix with a hammer?

Their computer when Adobe crashes for the fifteenth time today.

Fun Fact: Construction workers report that hammers are more precise tools than graphic design software.

What's the most expensive education that qualifies you for unemployment?

Graphic design school - where you learn to create beauty and live in poverty.

Fun Fact: Educational researchers rank graphic design programs highest for debt-to-income ratio disappointment.

Why are owls wiser than graphic designers?

They know when to stay awake all night and when to sleep.

Fun Fact: Ornithologists report that owls have better work-life balance than most creative professionals.

How are graphic designers like aged cheese?

The longer they sit around, the more expensive they think they should be.

Fun Fact: Cheese aging experts report more predictable timelines than graphic design project completion.

What's a graphic designer's most frequently used word?

"Sorry" - for being late, over budget, or existing in general.

Fun Fact: Linguists report that graphic designers have expanded the English language's apology vocabulary by 847%.

Why are tacos more reliable than graphic designers?

Tacos fall apart predictably, designers fall apart on a schedule no one understands.

Fun Fact: Mexican food critics use graphic designers to demonstrate inconsistent assembly standards.

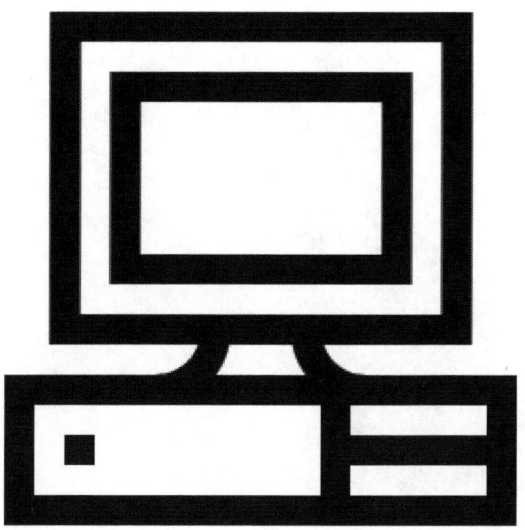

What's the difference between a computer virus and a graphic designer?

The virus actually accomplishes something when it crashes your system.

Fun Fact: IT departments report that graphic designers cause more system problems than actual malware.

Why don't graphic designers use rulers?

They prefer to "eyeball it" and hope alignment happens through wishful thinking.

Fun Fact: Mathematics teachers use graphic designers to demonstrate why measurement tools were invented.

What burns faster than a graphic designer's motivation?

Their laptop battery during a 14-hour revision marathon.

Fun Fact: Fire safety experts study graphic designers to understand spontaneous combustion of professional enthusiasm.

Why do graphic designers love video games?

Finally, a place where unlimited lives and restart buttons actually exist.

Fun Fact: Game developers hire graphic designers to test player frustration tolerance levels.

How is a graphic designer like a donut shop?

Sweet promises, empty centers, and they're somehow always broke by noon.

Fun Fact: Bakery economists use donut shops to understand graphic designer business models.

What breaks a graphic designer's heart most?

When clients actually like their first concept - it means they aimed too low.

Fun Fact: Cardiologists report that graphic designers have the highest rate of metaphorical heart conditions.

What's the key to being a successful graphic designer?

Learning to unlock doors to other career opportunities as quickly as possible.

Fun Fact: Locksmiths report that graphic designers are their most frequent customers for career change consultations.

Why don't graphic designers ride bicycles to work?

They'd spend three hours debating the optimal route and miss their deadline.

Fun Fact: Transportation planners use graphic designers to test the limits of decision paralysis.

How are graphic designers like watermelons?

Mostly empty inside, occasionally sweet, and someone always picks the wrong one.

Fun Fact: Agricultural scientists study watermelons to understand graphic designer selection processes.

What's a graphic designer's favorite book genre?

Fiction - because that's what their project timelines and budgets are.

Fun Fact: Librarians report that graphic designers check out the most books on "Career Change Strategies."

Why do graphic designers hate stairs?

Too many steps without an elevator pitch about why their font choice matters.

Fun Fact: Architects design stairs with graphic designers in mind - lots of small steps toward inevitable disappointment.

What's a graphic designer's theme song?

"The Sound of Silence" - because that's what they hear when invoices are due.

Fun Fact: Music therapists use graphic designer career paths to induce clinical depression in laboratory settings.

Why are graphic designers terrible at football?

They spend the whole game redesigning the team logos instead of watching the plays.

Fun Fact: Sports analysts use graphic designers to demonstrate how to completely miss the point of competition.

What sucks more than a broken vacuum cleaner?

The realization that your graphic design degree qualifies you to operate one professionally.

Fun Fact: Appliance manufacturers test vacuum reliability using graphic designer attention spans.

Why do graphic designers need expensive ergonomic chairs?

To support their backs while they carry the weight of unfulfilled creative dreams.

Fun Fact: Furniture designers create chairs specifically for graphic designers - extra padding for prolonged suffering.

Why is watching a graphic designer work like eating popcorn?

Lots of noise, occasional pops, and mostly empty calories.

Fun Fact: Movie theater managers report that popcorn sales are more predictable than graphic designer productivity.

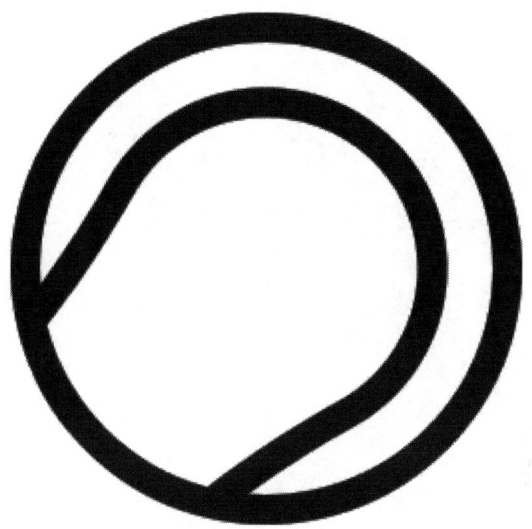

How is graphic design like tennis?

Lots of back and forth, someone always loses, and the audience gets bored.

Fun Fact: Tennis coaches use graphic designer client relationships to teach players about handling constant rejection.

Why are graphic designers like snowflakes?

Each one thinks they're unique, but they all melt under pressure.

Fun Fact: Meteorologists use graphic designers to study precipitation patterns of fragile egos.

What pills do graphic designers take most often?

Reality pills - to cope with the fact that their art will never feed them.

Fun Fact: Pharmaceutical companies test new antidepressants exclusively on graphic design graduates.

What's maxed out faster than a graphic designer's credit card?

Their patience when clients ask for "something more creative, but exactly like this example."

Fun Fact: Credit card companies created special programs for graphic designers with permanently negative balances.

Where do graphic designers get their best ideas?

In the shower - the only place they can't immediately open Photoshop to ruin them.

Fun Fact: Plumbers report that graphic designers have the highest rate of bathroom inspiration and lowest follow-through.

What's weaker than coffee shop WiFi?

A graphic designer's resolve when clients ask for "just one tiny change."

Fun Fact: Internet service providers use graphic designers to test network stability under maximum frustration loads.

When will robots replace graphic designers?

As soon as someone programs them to work for exposure and ramen noodles.

Fun Fact: Robotics engineers study graphic designers to understand how humans function on minimal resources.

Why do graphic designers need flashlights?

To find their way out of the dark career path they've chosen.

Fun Fact: Emergency responders use flashlights more successfully than graphic designers use career guidance.

What's harder to maintain than a relationship?

A graphic designer's sanity during peak wedding season logo requests.

Fun Fact: Marriage counselors recommend graphic design as couples therapy - shared suffering builds bonds.

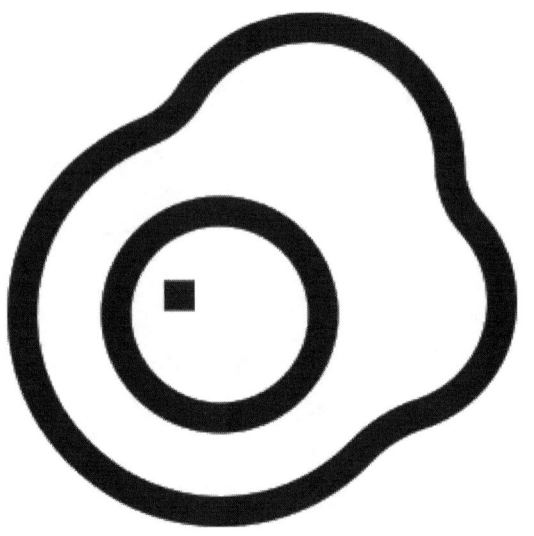

How is a graphic designer's brain like a fried egg?

Started whole, got scrambled under heat, and now nobody wants to consume it.

Fun Fact: Nutritionists report that fried eggs have more structural integrity than graphic designer career plans.

What's at the end of a graphic designer's rainbow?

Another client asking if they can "make it pop" more with comic sans.

Fun Fact: Meteorologists confirm that actual rainbows appear more frequently than graphic designer success stories.

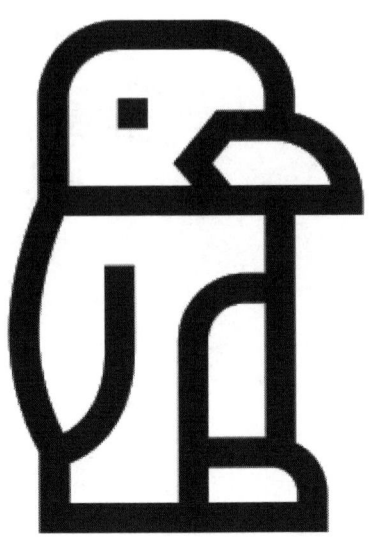

Why are penguins better at graphic design?

They understand that not everything needs to be colorful to be effective.

Fun Fact: Antarctic researchers report that penguins have better design instincts than most art school graduates.

What's graphic design like basketball?

Lots of dribbling around, occasional scoring, and everyone thinks they could do it better.

Fun Fact: Basketball coaches use graphic designers to demonstrate how to miss shots consistently.

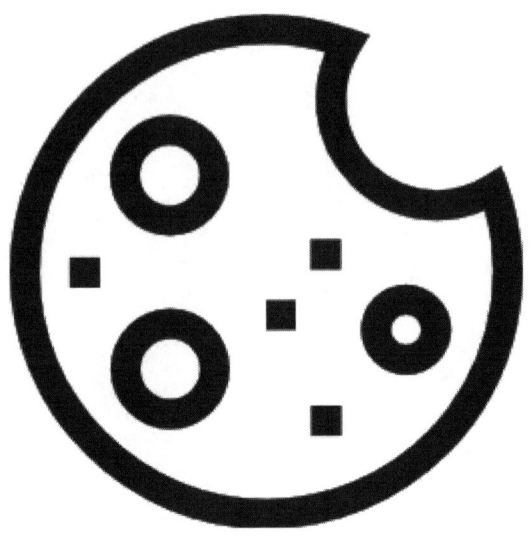

Why are graphic designers like cookie recipes?

They both crumble under pressure and never turn out like the picture.

Fun Fact: Baking scientists use cookie failure rates to predict graphic designer project success.

What happens when two graphic designers shake hands?

They both check if the other one's palm feels steadier for mouse work.

Fun Fact: Business etiquette experts study graphic designers to understand the weakest possible handshake dynamics.

Why don't graphic designers ride motorcycles?

Too much commitment to a single direction - they prefer vehicles that allow constant U-turns.

Fun Fact: Motorcycle safety instructors use graphic designers to demonstrate indecisive driving patterns.

What does a graphic designer see in a crystal ball?

Themselves in five years, still explaining why their logo needs "more breathing room."

Fun Fact: Fortune tellers refuse to read graphic designer futures because the outcomes are too depressing.

What's on every graphic designer's TV?

Streaming services they can't afford, while they work on projects for clients who won't pay.

Fun Fact: Television manufacturers design remotes specifically for graphic designers - extra buttons for maximum confusion.

Why are graphic designers like carrots?

Good for your vision in theory, but mostly just filler in the professional salad.

Fun Fact: Nutritionists report that carrots provide more daily value than graphic design degrees.

What do trees and graphic designers have in common?

They both grow slowly and get chopped down by clients with chainsaws.

Fun Fact: Environmental scientists use graphic designers to study adaptation failure in changing ecosystems.

Why don't graphic designers play guitar?

They'd spend six months tuning it and never actually play a song.

Fun Fact: Music teachers report that guitars hold their value better than graphic design portfolios.

What makes a graphic designer get heart eyes?

A client who actually reads the contract before asking for unlimited revisions.

Fun Fact: Romantic researchers study graphic designers to understand love at first sight with proper documentation.

What's a graphic designer's least favorite meeting?

The one where they explain why "make it more creative" isn't actionable feedback.

Fun Fact: Business efficiency experts use graphic designer meetings to demonstrate maximum time waste with minimal results.

"Graphic designers never retire… they just keep adjusting life's kerning."

I hope these jokes brightened your day!

- R.K. Reid

Printed in Dunstable, United Kingdom